Asmaa BAGHLI

Unspoken Words

AF135590

Asmaa BAGHLI

Unspoken Words

32 Love Poems

JustFiction Edition

Publisher:
JustFiction! Edition
is a trademark of
Dodo Books Indian Ocean Ltd. and OmniScriptum S.R.L publishing group

120 High Road, East Finchley, London, N2 9ED, United Kingdom
Str. Armeneasca 28/1, office 1, Chisinau MD-2012, Republic of Moldova, Europe
Printed at: see last page
ISBN: 978-620-0-10459-5

Collection of 32 Poems

I hereby thank all people who believed in me,
all those who inspired me!

Table of Content

"The truth never Told"

when there is no hand to hold,
when the truth is there but never told,
when hearts are alive but cold,
and young people look old,
when a nice person is sold,
cheaply though having heart of gold,
when language becomes a code,
and interpretation is unavowed
Only then could you say,
Goodbye for today,
some people are not supposed to stay,
others for the pain they cause will pay,
playing with soft-hearted people is mean,
pretending kindness is unclean
peace be upon the world,
if there is no honest word,
if the soul easily succumb,
to death, instead of believing in fate!

"Little Lilacs Flower"

Under the shade of the 🌳 tree,
grows the little lilacs flower,
takes cover from the hot sun,
from rain and cold weather,
I would stay here forever,
said the tree to the flower,
I will cover you with my branches,
so there are few chances,
that you get sick or die,
you'll ever look into my eye,
and contemplate the blue sky,
in a soft calm voice and shy,
the little flower tempts to reply,
you're the reason I'm alive,
without your branches and leaves 🌿
I wouldn't have survived,
No little flower,
it's you that gives me the power,
to standstill in my place,
your existence is my grace,
so I set the pace
for your safety,
Just keep being beautiful and tasty !

"True Love"

Love
is beyond those simple words to say,
it should not be something to play,
or joke with then threw away,

I reckon ...
Sometimes, God gives it to you as gift,
it let your soul slowly drift,
you don't know why you love,
or why you can't put someone else's above,
Still, one has to be rational,
there are things unnatural,
Different is our perception,
though there's unusual connection,
dissimilar is our conception,
You seem to have no direction,
and have sundry interceptions,
the difference is clear,
while the reason is near !
it would rapidly dissappear !

Dear fisher bird,
Fly high in the blue sky,
You are not anyone to deny,
Send my greetings to my .....
in this hot sunny summer,
Holding such a beautiful flower,
in that stunning ... color,
with its magical power,
tell them gently "Hello"

I have something for you to show,

give them that flower and go,

it will help them so,

They won't say No,

they'll soon know,

the truth they've missed years ago,

they've been living though,

they've missed the beautiful snow,

"I wish ..."

I wish ...

I could go back with time,
when everything was fine,
peaceful divine mind,

If Only...

I could see through my eyes,
Considering all the lies,
before time flies,
and I'll be such an unwise,

I wish...
I could turn back the clock ⏰
never allowed....to mock,
at my little rational mind,
and try to read what lies behind,
playfulness, unrighteousness, that kind,
of person, on the forehead signed,
But such a candid was I and blind,

If Only...
I could take back my words,
but gone are the birds,
I could change my way,
repaint my cold gray sky,
utterly delete that day,
cancel what I did say,
leave...as ...wanted to play,
and take myself and move away,
for there's no need to stay,

"Mistake"

What kind of mistake is done?
Rationally speaking, I could see none,

or...maybe,
the heart shouldn't have run,
there was only darkness,not the sun,

now....
face the words that kill more than a gun,
the heart and the mind should be one,
believing...was the mistake,
little did I know how perfectly fake,
could the person be..as if a snake,
utterly nice, polite, from outside,
desperately Unrighteous, cold inside,

It takes days thinking,
how can we be sinking,
in darkness and happily singing..?
an excuse worse than a sin,
but now I believe the saying
straight trees ♠ are always chosen for cutting

"Mistake"

Could it be a lesson?
or such a false impression?
is there still any question ?
will come the day of confession?

what if he comes back,
and innocence drops from his eyes,
the mind is clearly black ,
Non could deny the fact,
only thunder, and lies,
that was the big surprise,
gone is the innocent soul,
a wide flood of lies, out of control,

how could the soul forgive,
how can she, in anyone, believe,
broken is the trust,
gone with the dust,
it's such unjust,
lifted are the pens

dried are the books,
there come their ends,
it meant more than it looks,
if innocence was drops of water ●,

it would stained with sinners blood,
if the good word was magic,
it would lost its beauty,
fake masks have fallen off,
all the cards are played,
what goes around, comes around,

God will repay for the pain
only the good word will remain,

"Just a Dream"

Dreaming of
the green spaces that never dry
all together and aiming high,
where time would never fly,
contemplating the stunning blue sky,
lovely pure spirit would never die
loving is free; not to to beg for neither to buy
happy couples, no one to cry
hopes never dimmed, shining bright eyes,
good men, beautiful women but shy
the truth is there not to deny,
all things are clear, never wondering why,
living with honesty, sincerity, no lie,
being together, no one to say goodbye !

"Broken"

Broken is the hand given,

to help, with no one to listen,

pulling it deep down

throwing the princess's crown,

no previous reason found,

Still, standing its ground,

objecting to be drown,

in the sea of its false perception,

It was indeed a reflection,

of only a pure intention

but set to the wrong direction !

"Beauty and the Beast"

Among all the handsome men,

Once, twice, time and again,

choosing him with a reason,

in the cold- hot winter season,

She is beautiful with female dominance,

Intelligent, speaking in confidence

brave , courageous and true

knows what she wants, she's a clear view !

He is the hidden adventure,

unique in its gender,

rough, harsh but has potential,

that's her foremost essential,

she civilises him,

that was in the film,

Disney beauty and the beast,

At the end, no one is born a priest!

"Silent Broken"

Not the heart that is broken,

but the naive expectations,

the mind is awoken,

with Clear limitations,

the soul is still open,

to another alternation,

Leaving.....for his lies,

is like leaving the country for its rain,

liars nowadays are getting prize,

it rains everywhere, time and again,

From now on, open your eyes,

then preserve your heart

for liars are becoming wise !

so be smart !

"Blind !"

maybe that wasn't my place,

maybe that time wasn't my time,

time to look for another space,

or simply go back to your precious race,

maybe my imagination took me,

to another planet that was too far,

I failed though to see,

how true people are !!

what was the cost at the end,

apart from feeling lost,

"Grey !"

It's grey,

It's cold

there's no other way,

no truth is to be told,

no time to play,

the truth gets enfold,

we just realize today,

It's hard to find gold,

kindness is easy to display,

characters hard to mould,

thoughts ready to betray,

emotions quickly sold !

feeling peaceful today,

for the inner beauty we hold !

"New Sweetness!"

when sweetness disappears,

when God is real, but no fear,

when having two ears, but no ear,

when truthfulness is not here,

when prayers are sent, Only God to hear,

when consciousness is never to appear,

when everything is crystal clear,

when prayers wipe out tears,

only then could we say,

what's done is done,

honest, pure souls are gone,

sweet lies are transparent,

irrational minds are apparent,

it's not our time ,

l.... nowadays is a crime,

but there is a sunnier clime

for anyone who is true,

it will come one day out of blue!

"Hello December !"

Hello December,
happy that you're here,
sweetness is getting closer,
what are your plans for the new year?
tenderness is pouring over,
hot-cold hearts to hear,
inner soft roaring lover,
is suddenly to appear,
th rain's drops cleaning hearts to recover,
making it perfectly crystal clear,
souls would unconsciously surrender,
to the warmth of the snowfire adhere,
it's time to be happy and warm over ,
time to smile and be near,
,it's time to dote on, be the sower ,
be to your present a good ear !

"Forgotten !"

Forgotten...
you will be ,
as never been present,
Forgotten...
as a killed bird,
never again will it be seen,
forgotten...
as a passing love,
nothing pure is seemigly pleasant !
No more good Morning
neither sweet words hearing!
the sun is never rising
not even to one word,
no need to drink water from the sea,
to réalise that it is salty !

"Never Knew !"

that time I never knew,

things... said weren't true,

all the pain I've been through,

you have absolutely no clue !

you did not clarify your view,

neither wanted to review,

what you've done is not new,

you're used to play, throw too !

what's done is done,

what's said is said,

what's left is gone,

just run instead,

you thought it's fun,

while it made me sad,

hurted more than one,

that what made you glad,

your words are such a gun,

my mind is already mad ,

If you think I'll forgive then,

you're wrong, your soul is dead !

your presence was something,

but your absence meant everything,

.I can hold my hand by myself,

no need to have another shelf,

"Heart Sold !"

in a time when,

the truth is never to be told,

fake kindness is such a gold,

pure hearts are forever sold,

minds are rough and bold,

a soul into playing enrolled,

regret in a burnt blanket fold,

eyes in disbelief rolled,

a wrong sight to behold,

honesty is rarely hold,

the harsh truth is exposed,

no one is to be owned,

it's this way ,a vicious code,

solid bumpy tricky rode,

conscious for the wrong choice scoled,

The cost is already foretold,

truthfulness is not upon him bestowed!

"New Year !"

it's a new year,

everything is so far clear

than what it used to appear,

it's no more an interesting sphere,

it's totally a closed book,

no more time to take a look,

new papers empty and white,

a right pen ready to write,

with completely a different sight,

the story of a new vision

coming out of a decision,

with no more revision,

but only one condition,

it's either the good way

or the High way,

there is no time to delay,

so let's start today ☺

"Gone the Loving Spring !"

Gone is the loving spring,
it's the winter season,
the bird has lost its wings,
the coldness is the reason,
feelings onto the air cling,
honesty is in prison!
mastery of playing games,
nastiness is served and eaten !
the sky with stones rains,
on a fake soul unspoken,
thunder of regret resound the brain,
for the wrong option chosen,
it's a vicious sandy lake,
that killed motions then frozen,
how would the mind awake,
if insincerity was the token !

"Does Love Sleep !"

does love sleep at night,
or the night sleeps lovely,
or love, night and me sleep together?
do we need some red light,
or enough for us to be bubbly,
admiring profoundly in a soft weather,
tenderness is flooded in delight,
fondness is raining slowly,
appreciating that unique treasure,
we are ready to take our flight,
passion strummed chord gently,
admiring the beauty like never,
hearts are pure, souls are white,
devotion flowing like waterfalls solely,
Today, tonight, tomorrow and forever!

"Not Yours!"

what is not for you
will never be yours,
even if you hope to,
it's not a matter of choice,
honest people are nowadays few,
insincerity has a strong voice,
it's not something new,
to meet only boys,
acting a man like is true,
only if beliefs are pure,
be yourself and sincere though,
everyone will pay one day for sure !

"Impossible !"

it's impossible,

not even imaginable,

too far is the sky,

only common birds fly by ,

I thought I found myself,

but I was the man in action,

I'd remove it from the shelves,

it's such a wrong assumption,

different is our rains,

passed are our trains,

it's not the same mud,

nor the same blood,

I am a modest walking veil,

not available for every male,

you're a walking loud bell,

easy to reach and to sell,

no one ever lived on the moon,

it's definitely a different tune,

and we slowly become immune !

"Maybe !"

Maybe ...
it would have been better,
not to drink from sea water,
and to choose rather sugar!

Maybe...
I had to go that way,
the sky had to be grey,
to find my sunshine ray ,

Maybe...
My assumptions were wrong,
it was not there were I belong,
and that was only a lying song,

Maybe...
feelings wasn't what he deserves,
his heart is a reversed curves,
unconsciousness never swerves,

Maybe...
he wouldn't cost a dime,
loving him was a crime,
or you're born in the wrong time,

Maybe...
it's now your day,
to sing and play,
because everything will be okay!

"What if..?!"

what if..
the book is written again,
the pen is never to refrain,
souls are happy, no pain,
we are all there to remain,

what if..
we both signed in,
no one around to spin,
lost time is never to begin,
the one eternal truth is within,

what if...
the seas met,
no-one would get wet,
we've paid all our debt,
sands are clean and set,

what if...
the shadow spoke,
I'm alive thanks to the oak,
the heat you did soak,
and warmth you provoke,

what if...
the sunrises is forever there,
happiness is beyond compare,
breathing tenderness' air,
we're aware and ready to share !

"Sleep my Pearl !"

sleep quietly in my arms,
no one would harm you

I am here...
the world turns around,
still no way you'll feel blue,

I am here...
the noisy harsh people's sound,
my heart to you remains true,

I am here...
Your glory was hard to find,
you bring in me everything new,

I am here...
forever with you dear,
have no fear,
everything will be fine, near,

I am here...
you're the protagonist in my story,
you are my secret and my glory,

Just...
Grew up honest, clean and sincere !

"Frosty Winter !"

A warm frosty winter,

A soft cold breath,

Souls merged as tinder,

Around love passionate Candlelight!

Thrilling long fairy tales,

Following affectionate voice trails!

Soft tone whispering,

Glory eyes sparkling,

Pure hearts flickering,

Little lovely angels,

Unlikely to swap the channel,

Devotion is pouring;

Not to be covered up,

Tenderness is roaring,

Laughter out of them bubbling up

Eating sweetness,

Relishing mind's neatness,

Savouring uniqueness,

No time for feeling bitter,

It is the beauty of the winter!

"Tell them ..."

Tell them ...

How much you are precious

How you are incredibly courageous,

Tell them ...

You are my only heart,

Never will we fall apart,

Tell them ...

You are my lovely world,

My little smart bird,

Tell them ...

You are my history but my present,

Vivid soul and effervescent,

You are my positive energy provision,

My past present rational decision,

And my future vision!

"Tell them ..."

Why is the good thrown away

Why is nectar flowers stolen,

is it the rule of the day,

To crash and leave unspoken!

The sky is raining in goodness,

While Humanity is being eroded,

Little flowers fading of sadness,

Human's mental abuse flooded!

Appearances invading the place,

Minds in a time forgotten,

Fake smile on the face,

Unclean soul never open!

Little do we realise the truth,

For the veracity is never awoken!

But days are not forever grey,

It was only a drop in the ocean !

"You Decided ..."

What I've asked for,

Is not something you can give,

Never required more,

But you've chosen to leave!

You've preferred to ignore,

And I decided not to forgive !

You've closed the door,

And I've chosen to freely live !

You have thrown it on the floor,

And I have learnt how to sieve,

you like to play and explore,

and I picked the moment to relive !

the lesson I have learnt !

The person I forgot !

The shadow has been burnt

Just move on and put a dot !

"Valentine Day"

It is such a beautiful day,

Mysterious Tenderness is around

Only devotion is to display,

On a clear soft green ground,

No one is here to play,

Affection is to be crowned,

Gazing eyes show more than say,

Adoration flame from eyes could sound,

Fondness could not be shown other way,

For true love is so profound,

We are here forever to stay,

Hearts' beat truly pound,

Faithfulness on our promises would lay,

You are the best I have ever found!

The sky will never be grey,

This is what we have avowed,

Everything will be okay,

This is what we have vowed,

True love is not a passing cloud,

Say it out and loud!

"Not the Pain!"

It is not the pain that hurts ,

Nor the heart flames that burns,

Neither the fake rules that alert,

Not even the intention reversed,

It is how unjust you were,

 Fake kindness in a dirty air,

Absent conscious and no care,

Harshness and no one fair!

I wish I were not there !

"I do Not want to Remember!"

I do not want to remember

But couldn't stop thinking

I am a woman of slender,

Echoes are still winking,

How could I be so wrong?

And I am the one who knows gold from silk

It was a joke ghost passing song,

And only fake words to drink,

I blame myself maybe

I atone for a sin I did not commit,

It looks like I am still a baby,

To allow my mind to submit,

Why does thistle grow

around a simple innocent flower?

And cold air on the heart blew,

As a freezing bloody shower!

None of the rational reasons is logical,

None could explain the impossible,

Sea and coral do not meet,

Not even in a dark street,

Even if it looks like sweet,

We all have feet of clay,

Bu never did I intend to play,

Yet none of us is forever to stay,

Each will find his way,

Still…

I wish I never met you that day!